PROOFING IS IN THE PUDDING
Recipes to Correct and Cook

written by Julia Ring Alarie and Elizabeth Conlon
illustrated by Priscilla Burris

AF207116

JULIA RING ALARIE received a Bachelor of Arts degree from Trinity College in Burlington, Vermont. She is an experienced language arts teacher in Essex Center, Vermont.

ELIZABETH CONLON received a Bachelor of Arts degree in French from Trinity College and a Master of Arts degree in Teaching English as a Second Language from St. Michael's College in Winooski, Vermont. She is a language arts teacher in Essex Center, Vermont.

PRISCILLA BURRIS received an Associate of Arts degree in Creative Design from the Fashion Institute of Design and Merchandising in Los Angeles. As a free-lance artist of child-related artwork, she has been drawing since she was one year old. Priscilla lives in southern California.

Reproduction of these pages by the classroom teacher for use in the classroom and not for commercial use is permissible. Reproduction of these pages for an entire school or school system is strictly prohibited.

Copyright 1983 by THE MONKEY SISTERS, INC.
22971 Via Cruz
Laguna Niguel, CA 92677

PROOFING IS IN THE PUDDING

The skills involved in proofreading are introduced in this lively series of lessons by Carmen Cuisine of "The Cooking with Carmen Show," a fictitious TV cooking show.

Carmen's recipes are easily followed once the spelling, punctuation, grammar and capitalization have been corrected.

The format is simple and fun. Students read the introduction and the recipe and then re-write the recipe on the card below. These are actual recipes children can create and cook. Additional activity pages giving practice in sequencing, categorizing, sentence structure and review are included.

For added motivation, try preparing some of the recipes in class allowing students to bring in utensils and ingredients. Students may also want to dramatize the lesson by "becoming" Carmen for the lesson.

For extra credit, students can be encouraged to start their own cookbook using Carmen's Cards. They may be graded for:
—creative design of their cookbook
—neatness
—organization
—creative title

CONTENTS

Letters following page title indicate skills emphasized.

S = spelling   **P** = punctuation   **C** = capitalization   **G** = grammar
Q = sequencing   **V** = abbreviation   **A** = addresses   **T** = sentence structure
F = following directions   **Z** = categorizing

ISBN 0-933606-22-2

Dear Student,

I am so pleezed to meat you! My name is Carmen, and I host the weekly TV cooking show, "The Cooking with Carmen Show."

As you will find out, I am quiet a good cook, but I do have problemz riding out my recipes correctly. I'll be happy to share the secrits of my top recipes with you, but in order to injoy them, you will have to correct them.

Save the recipe cards and start your very own cookbook with Carmen's Cards.

Happy cooking and happy correcting, too!

CARMEN

Re-write my letter as neatly as you can.

____

____

____

____

____

____

____

____

SAFETY RULES FOR
THE KITCHEN

I often remember the wise advice of my cooking instructor, Professor Cooke. Here are the notes I took during Professor Cooke's lecture titled: "Carful Cooks Cook Carfully"

Proofread my notes and copy them over correctly. You may want to add them to your recipe file for safety tips.

1. Allways use potholders to hold hot pots.

   ____

2. Do'nt where lose cloths near stove burnors.

   ____

3. Keep a fire extinguishor near the stove.

   ____

4. Whipe up spils on floor immediately.

   ____

5. Turn all pot handels tward the back of the stove.

   ____

6. Rember steem can burn you, two.

   ____

7. Refrigerate perishable food when not being used.

   ____

8. Store food tightely coverd so bugs cant get in.

   ____

9. Warsh hands befor you handel any food.

   ____

10. Be careful of sharp instraments.

   ____

Proofing is in the Pudding © THE MONKEY SISTERS, INC.

APPLE PANCAKES

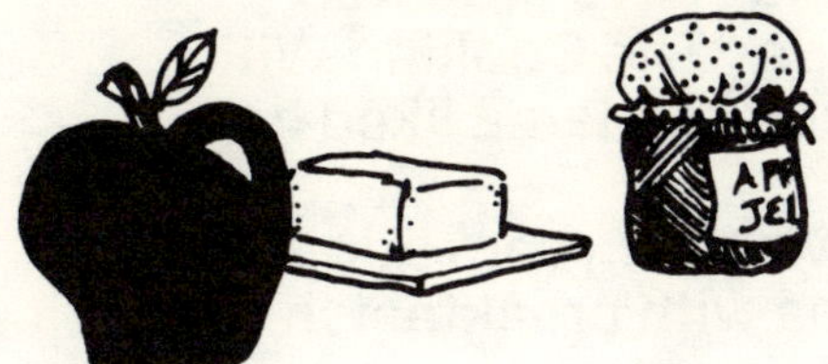

Got those What's For Breakfast Blues?
The "Cooking With Carmen Show" comes to the
rescue with **Pan-Fried Apple Wedges**, a delicious
topping for breakfast pancakes.

Start your day right
With each yummy bite!

Ingredents:

2 read cooking appels, cored
2 tabelspoons butter or margerine
1/2 cup appel jelley

Directions:

1. Cut apple in 1/2-inch thick weges.

2. In 12 inch skillit over meduim heat, in hot butter or margerine, cook appel weges
   about 5 too 7 minutes untill apple are tender (turn weges once during cooking).

3. Stir in appel jelley; heat threw. Serve over warm pancakes. Makes 4 servings.

Name ____

Proofing is in the Pudding © THE MONKEY SISTERS, INC.

BAKED BREAKFAST SURPRISE

Every year since we were very young, my sister and I have prepared breakfast for our Mama on Mother's Day. Today on "The Cooking With Carmen Show," I am going to share one of the recipes Mama liked best.

I seem to have made some mistakes when I first wrote it years ago. Please copy it over before you surprise your Mama with breakfast in bed.

BAKED EGGS (one serving)

You need: an egg
      1 tsp. milk
      1 tbsp. shredded chease

Buter a custerd cup.
Carfully brake in to eggs
Add one teasespoon milk.
Sit cup in pan in ovon.
Poor hot watter in pan.
Back at 325° for 10 minits.
Sprinkel eggs whith one tabelspon shreded chease.
Back for 15 more minits untill eggs are firm.

Name

Proofing is in the Pudding © THE MONKEY SISTERS, INC.

CREAMY ORANGE SMOOTHIE
(an A.M. OJ Treat!)

The weather outside is frightful
But your breakfast was so delightful!
You know it will help you grow,
'Cause you saw it on "The Cooking With Carmen Show"!

Yes, you're having a beautiful morning because you made a Creamy Orange Smoothie for breakfast. In my rush, I forgot to put the directions in order. Once you do this, you'll have another great recipe for your file.

Ingredience: frozen 6 oz. orange juice
milk cup 1½
cup ½ water
sugar cup ¼
½ vanilla teaspoon
10 ice cubes
2 egg

Directions: serve immediately
blend until smooth and cover
place all ingredience in blender
makes 2-3 servings

Don't forget to put away the ingredients and to clean up!

Name

Proofing is in the Pudding © THE MONKEY SISTERS, INC.

AFTER SCHOOL TRIPLE TREAT

Today, I'm going to show you how to prepare three quick treats you can make with your friends after school. If you follow along with me, you'll be able to make them in no time. Here are the recipes, but please remember to correct them because, as usual, I was too busy cooking to be careful in writing them down! Remember, too, clean up after preparing your treats.

MARY SUE'S MILK SHAKE

Put the folling ingredients in blender and blend on hi for 1 min.
   1 cup milk
   2 scops cholocate ice creme
   1 tablesppon hony
   2 ice cubs
Serve.

PETE'S P.B.&B. SANDWICH

Tost 2 slice of bread.
Slice up ripe banana.
Spred peanutt buter on both slices of tost.
Palce sliced bananana in between and make sandwich.
Injoy!

STEVE'S STUFED SELERY

Clean 8 stalks of selery.
Fill each with penut buter.
Sprinkel with bakon bits.
Serves for!

Name

Proofing is in the Pudding © THE MONKEY SISTERS, INC.

CHOCOLATE CRACKER SNACKER

Announcing the Carmen Cuisine Remarkable Rebate

Here's all you have to do to receive the C.C.R. REBATE. Simply follow these directions perfectly. Then hand in this paper to your teacher.

1. Cross out the misspelled words and put the correct spelling above each word.

2. Circle any misplaced words in the entire recipe.

3. Put a box □ around any punctuation that isn't needed.

4. Put in any punctuation that is needed and is missing.

5. Underline any errors in grammar.

Surprize a freind whith Carmens Choklit Cracker Snaker a desert easy and nutritious

    1 tbsp cream cheese
    1 tsp, milk
    ½ tsp, sugar
    1/8 tsp, coco

Beat the cheese with the milk untill smooth then beaten in sugar and coco spread on gram craker

---

This Rebate valid only when signed by Carmen Cuisine and your teacher.

Carmen Cuisine

CARMEN CUISINE'S REMARKABLE REBATE

issued to: _______________________

FOR OUTSTANDING PROOFREADING.

Value: _______________________
(to be filled in by teacher)
Teacher: _____________ Date: __________

Proofing is in the Pudding © THE MONKEY SISTERS, INC.

A DIRECTOR'S DILEMMA!

Mona Templeton, the director of "The Cooking With Carmen Show," has timed the second half of the show and realizes Carmen will only have a few minutes to explain this recipe. Many of the sentences in the directions could be combined. Waste no time in proofreading these directions!

CARROT-RAISIN SALAD

2 carrots
2 apples
1 stalk of celery
½ cup raisins
¼ tsp. salt
1 tsp. lemon juice

½ c. mayonnaise, sour cream,
   or yogurt
¼ cup chopped nuts
lettuce leaves

Serves 4.

Wash the carrots. Grate the carrots. Wash the apples. Do not peel them. Cut them in half. Cut them in quarters. Cut out the core. Cut the apples in small pieces.

Wash the celery. Chop the celery. Add the celery to the carrots. Add the apples to the carrots. Add the raisins to the carrots. Sprinkle with salt and lemon juice.

Stir in mayonnaise. Or stir in sour cream. Or stir in yogurt. Serve salad on lettuce leaves and sprinkle with nuts.

Name ___________________

Proofing is in the Pudding © THE MONKEY SISTERS, INC.

HONEY CRUNCH PEANUT SPREAD
(unbearably delicious)

Fred Eclair can't concentrate on his social studies today. All he can think about is the super treat he's got in his lunch box. It was just yesterday that he saw this treat prepared on my show. It sure looked good to Fred. He copied the recipe but forgot to make the corrections. Would you proofread it and make the corrections for Fred? He'll be so happy!

Ingredient: 1¼ c. p. buter
         *⅔ c. toast oats
         ½ c. huny
         ½ c. raisons
         ½ c. semisweet cholate chips

*first make toast oats:

   Put Quaker oats on ungrease cooky sheet.
   Bake at 350 degrees for 15-20 or til golden browned
   cool
   Store in tight covered container in refrigerator.

How to make spread:

Combine all ingredients mix well store in closed container in refrigerator serve as sandwich spread on creachers or with carrot stix

Name

MIDNIGHT MILKSHAKE

Tonight, our regular program schedule has been changed and I am pleased to bring you this special late-night version of "The Cooking With Carmen Show."

Kevin Kantslepe is in desperate need of a bedtime snack. I was a little sleepy myself when I wrote this recipe so proofread it and copy it over correctly.

1 cup venella ice creme
1/2 cup milk

Plase venella ice creme in blendar container; ad milk. Cover. Blend untill mixchur is smoothe. Poor in to a glass. Serve immediatly. Sip slowley through a straw. Slepe tight!

Name

   Proofing is in the Pudding © THE MONKEY SISTERS, INC.

ROBOT RECIPE

The producers are considering hiring Robby, the robot, to be the new proofreader for "The Cooking With Carmen Show." But wait a minute! That's your job!!

Here is a sample of Robby's work. Prove that *you* are a better proofreader than the robot by proofreading Robby's corrections.

Copy the recipe over correctly.

Original Recipe: Bananana Snack Goes Nutie

> 1 ripe bananana
> 2 tabelspoons choped nuts

Spred nuts on a pece of wax papper. Peal bananana. Press the nuts in to the bananana so they stick all over. Place bananana in Frezer four one hour. Enjoye it!

Robby's Corrected Recipe: Bananna Snack Gose Nuddy

> 1 wripe bananna
> 2 tabelspoons choppet nutz

Spread nutz on a piece of wax papper. Pele bananna. Pres the nutx into the bananna so they stick alover. Place bananna in freezr for on hour. Injoy it!

Your Corrected Recipe:

Name

SEVEN STORY SANDWICH

I've come to your school to be the special guest hot lunch cook. Every student has written his favorite recipe and I've picked one to prepare for lunch today. Proofread it, so there will be no problem preparing a luscious lunch.

1. Toast english muffin
2. Spread 1/2 with mayonnaise
   1/2 with musterd

3. Layer on the following: letuce leaf
   baloney slice
   slice of cheese
   ham slice
   tomatoe slice

4. Top with other halves.

Serve with French fryes, milk, carrot, celery sticks, and fresh fruit.

Name ____________________

Proofing is in the Pudding © THE MONKEY SISTERS, INC.

YUMMY NUT and HONEY SANDWICH

Today on "The Cooking With Carmen Show" we have a very special guest, Ms. May Anaise, to help us prepare for the Annual Surprise Sandwich Picnic. May's Yummy Nut and Honey Sandwich will be a real treat at the picnic. (The recipe card should look as terrific as the sandwich itself!)

Correct the mistakes in the recipe and rewrite it on the recipe card.

**Yummy Nut
and Honey Sandwich**

2-3 tbspn. peanutt buter
1 stripe crispy bakon
1/2 teasp. huney
razin bred

Krumple bakon into peanutt buter than add huney mix together spread on warm razin bred makes too sandwichs holesum an nutrisious.

Name

FANSY FONEY FRENCH "FROG" LEGS

"Don't fret, Fricasse Frog, I'm not interested in you!
I've found this recipe instead. But you can help me by
proofreading it before I start cooking!"

Ingredience: 12 chiken wings
1/2 8-oz. bottle Etalian dressing

Directions: Cut the tips off the wings. Place wings on cooky
sheet. Sprinkle with salad dressing. Cover top with
alumimum foil an bake at 350 degrees for a hour. Makes
4 too 6 servings.

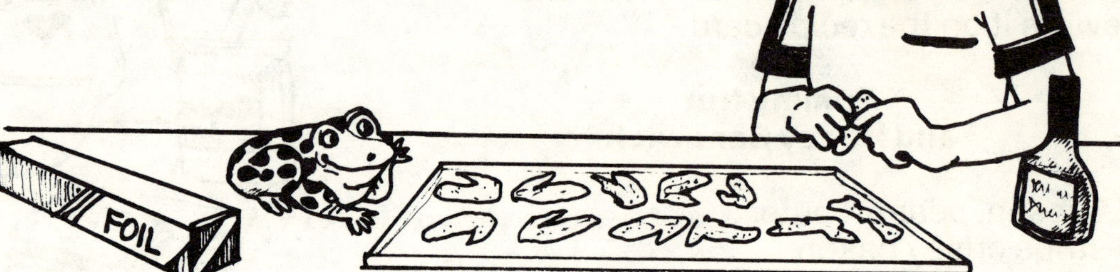

Name

   Proofing is in the Pudding © THE MONKEY SISTERS, INC.

MAMA MIA'S GARLIC BREAD

The special guest host on today's "Cooking With Carmen Show" is Mama Mia, who is widely known for her "Mama Mia's Garlic Bread." Our camerman, Anthony, has written the recipe on the cue cards, but there are mistakes. Before I let Mama Mia start cooking, correct the errors and copy the recipe neatly on the card.

Mama Mia's Garlic Bread

1 lofe italian bread (sliced in half lengthwise)
Spred budder on the bred
Top with slices of mozzarella cheese (do'nt be stingy!)
Sprinkel with garlic power and oregano
Place on cookie sheet and broil at 400° until cheese melts
Cut bred into serving peaces.
Serve with spageti, or soups, or whatever!

Mama Mia's Garlic Bread

Name

CARMEN'S EXOTIC HAM

Lights! Camera! Ac . . . Wait!! "The Cooking With Carmen Show" can't go on. I, Carmen Cuisine, have tried this recipe eight times, but it didn't come out right. It *can't* be my cooking, so it must be the directions. I need your help! NOW!! Please proof it. The show must go on!!

Youll need the following ingredience:

    1 slise ham for each person
    1 pinapple ring for each person
    hole wheat flower
    a pinsh of salt
    1/4 cup of sweet and suor sauce

fry the ham untill brown in a large sauce pan add the sweet and suor sauce and the pinapple simer in the pot untill the ham is tender thicken sauce with the flower add a pinsh of salt for taste.

cool for an our in the refrigerator and surve it chilled with whipped mash potatoes.

Circle the mistakes, then copy the corrected recipe on the recipe card below.

Something's Cooking . . .

Name

. . . In Carmen's Kitchen

Proofing is in the Pudding © THE MONKEY SISTERS, INC.

MAMA MARKLE'S MARVELOUS MEETLOFE

Every day, Ms. Hamel has her class watch "The Cooking With Carmen Show" on television. One student writes down the recipe of the day and gives everyone a copy. Today is Terry Corning's turn and he is having a terrible time! Would you please proofread his work?

Circle the errors in the recipe below. Copy the recipe over correctly.

Equipemint

1 lofe pan
1 large bole
1 cup of bred crums
1 large spoone
1 messuring cup
1 messuring spoone

Engrediants

1-1/2 pounds growND meet
1/2 cup of melk
1 eeg
1/4 cup catsup
2 tablespoones of houseradish

In a large bole, blend the eeg, melk, catsup, and houseradish. Stir in the bred crums. Mix in the growND meet until it is well blended. Put it in a lofe pan. Bake at 350° for 1 hour and 15 minutes.

If you put in one potatoe for each person, to bake with the meet lofe, all you will nede is a vegtabel to make a compleet meel.

Name

Proofing is in the Pudding © THE MONKEY SISTERS, INC.

QUICKIE DINNER QUICHE

125 Main Street
Springfield, Alaska
February 18th

Dear Carmen,
    Please send me a copy of the Quickie Quiche you prepared on your show of Tuesday, January 30th. It looked delicious and seemed easy to make. Thank you.

Sincerely,

Lola Souffle

Lola Souffle

P.S. I watch your show every chance I can!

Before I send Lola the recipe, correct the shorthand notes I made when I used the recipe on the show.

1 unbkd 9 pie shell
1/2 c diced chick
1-1/2 c shrded Swiss chse
3 eggs, slight beat
1-1/2 c mlk
1/2 tsp slt
1/4 tsp mace
dash pep
2 tbsp grtd Parm ches

Place chick in p. shl w. Swiss chse. Comb. eggs, mlk, slt, mce, & pep. Poor over chse. Sprink on Parm. chse. Bake at 375 for 30-35 M or til a nife comes out clean. Allow to stand 10 min bfor srvg.

Name

 Proofing is in the Pudding © THE MONKEY SISTERS, INC.

SOUP FOR SUPPER

Even when I was in my teens, I used to make dinner for my family very often. In the summertime, I would make open-faced meat sandwiches with a salad and soup. My family especially loved my corn soup, and it always amused me because it is so very simple to make.

Re-write this old recipe correctly and treat your family to it as I still do.

CREAMED CORN SOUP

1 large (17 oz. size) creemed corn for eech too people
the same ammount of milk

Pur the creemed corn in to a pot. Fil empty can with milk and ad to creemed corn. Mix to gether under meduim heet untill it jest begins to boil but do not let it boil. Serve hot.

Serve with open-face roost beef sanwich on rye bread and a fresh friut salad.

Everyone loves this easy and diffrent super!

Name

AUNT NETTIE'S DELIGHTFUL AND DELICIOUS DESSERT

The recipe I'm going to prepare today is one of my all-time favorites that my aunt used to make for me when I was a little girl. I still love it! It's easy and fun to make and soooooo good!

Ingrediants: 18 gramm crackers
1 package of chocolate pudding
whipped topping

add the required amount of milk and cook chocolate pudding according to directions on the box let it cool but keep it covered so the skin does not form arrange 9 gramm crackers on a large plate 3 crackers across by 3 crackers down like a tic tac toe board when pudding is somewhat cooled pour it over the crackers cover the pudding with 9 more gramm crackers pour on remaining pudding make sure all crackers are evenly covered with the delicious chocolate pudding refrigerate until cool serve by cutting into 9 squares add whipped topping when you serve

Whoops! I got so carried away with this recipe I forgot to start and stop my sentences. Well, as you copy this recipe onto the card, correct the directions. Start the sentences with capital letters and end them with periods.

Hope you enjoy the delicious dessert!

Name

Proofing is in the Pudding © THE MONKEY SISTERS, INC.

AUNTIE PEG'S OTEMEEL BARZ

Today on "The Cooking With Carmen Show" we will be making
a delicious treat that can be eaten anytime from breakfast to
bedtime. My great-aunt Margaret used to make these whenever
I visited her. I wrote down the recipe when I was very young.
Maybe you'd better proof read it.

Circle the errors in the recipe.
Copy the recipe correctly on the recipe card.

2 cups of oatmeel, uncooked
3/4 cup of broun shugar
1/2 cup (one stick) batter or margerin
dash of backing soda
1/2 cup of one of these: razins, nutts, coconutt, choklit chips

Boil shuger, batter, and backing soda. Add oatmeel and 1/2 cup
of one of the speshall things and blend. Spread mixchur in a well
greest 8' skwar pan. Bake at 350° for 10 minuts. Cut into bars wile
warm. Ideel for breakfist or snacks.

Name ____

Proofing is in the Pudding © THE MONKEY SISTERS, INC.

Lil Annie adores "The Carmen Show." She is submitting her favorite cookie recipe to Carmen. Proofread her letter and the recipe to make sure there are no mistakes.

COOKIE COOKING!

Deer Ms Carmen

Heres an idear i though youd like alot These hear cookies are alright in my book I figered other folks would like em to. Please think about passin on this recipe on your show.

A fan,

Lil Annie

P.S. I call em Westren Cookie Bonanza

Sift together 1 cup whole wheat flower 1/2 teaspoon salt 1 teaspoon backing powder and 1 teaspoon cimmamin. Add 1 cup rolled oats and 1 cup finally chopped apples.

Cream together 1/2 cup butter and 1 cup brown sugar. Add 1 beaten egg and 1 Tabelspoon milk

Combine dry ingredients and creamed mixture. Drop bye spoonfulls onto oild baking sheet Bake in preheated oven at 350 degrees for 12-15 minutes.

makes about 2 dozen cookies

Happy Trails To You—

Name

Proofing is in the Pudding © THE MONKEY SISTERS, INC.

SUNDAE SCENE

Betsy and Julie, the creative writing geniuses behind "The Cooking With Carmen Show," have *quickly* written a short sketch for an upcoming   segment. The scene needs to be proofread before it goes to the typists. Help Julie and Betsy by correcting the mistakes below.

The Cooking With Carmen Show (Scene 1/Take 1)

KIDS: Hey, Mom, what's for dessert?
MOM: Sundaes!
KIDS: Yea! Hot fudge? Marshmallow? Chocolate?
MOM: Surprise! It's Rhubarb-Waffle Sundae!
KIDS: Sounds different. (A bit disappointed.)
      What's in it?
MOM: 3/4 pound rhubarb, cut into 1-inch peaces (2 cups)
      1/4 cup sugar
      2 tablespoon water
      1/2 tsp. lemin juice
      1/4 tsp. salt
      1/4 tsp. ginjer
      4 froze waffle
      1 pint vanella icecream

Here's what you do:

In 2-quart saucepin over medum heat, heat rubard suger water lemin juice, salt and ginjer to boiling. Reduce heat too lo; cover and summer 5-10 minutes until rubard is tender.

Prepare frozen waffel as lable directs. Place each waffle on a desert place. Scoop a ball off icecream onto each waffle Spoon warm rubard sauce over icecream and waffles. Makes a tangy desert!

KID 1: Ill try one!
KID 2: Me to!
KID 3: Me three!
MOM: (to camra) Sundaes will never be the same (winks)!
(Fade out. Scene ends.)

Name

Proofing is in the Pudding © THE MONKEY SISTERS, INC.

MEET SPEEDY EATY!

You probably wonder where Speedy Eaty, our super superheroine, gets all her power. Well, she never misses "The Cooking With Carmen Show" where she gets ideas for nutritious snacks and meals. She follows my advice and makes sure she's getting food from the basic food groups.

Proofread the lists she's made and circle any misplaced items. Then copy the lists over and correct any spelling errors.

Fruits and Vegetables		**Breads and Cereals**	
pees	_____________	rolls	_____________
pares	_____________	rolled oats	_____________
potatoes	_____________	granolla	_____________
peeches	_____________	brownie	_____________
parcenips	_____________	rice puffs	_____________
parmesan	_____________	stufing	_____________
pizza	_____________	hole wheat	_____________
tomato	_____________	bran muffin	_____________

Milk and Cheeses		**Meat, Fish, Poulty and Beans**	
yougort	_____________	troute	_____________
cotage cheese	_____________	hamberger	_____________
yello squash	_____________	turky	_____________
butter	_____________	garbonzoes	_____________
sour cream	_____________	grapes	_____________
ice creme	_____________	anchoveys	_____________
minster cheese	_____________	scallops	_____________
cream cheese	_____________	fryed chicken	_____________

   Proofing is in the Pudding © THE MONKEY SISTERS, INC.

HOW-TO . . . HARD BOIL

Carmen Cuisine is going to teach these four gourmet chefs how to hard boil an egg perfectly every time. Obviously, Chefs Wok, Kettle, Skillet and Cooker are a bit doubtful. Carmen is a little nervous, too! Proofread her directions before she presents them.

1. Have eggs at room temperture. Cold eggs from an icey refrigerator may crack when they touch the water.

____

2. Put the eggs in a sausepan

____

3. Cuver them whith cold water

____

4. Cook over meduim heat untill water boiles.

____

5. Put a lid on the sausepan

____

6. Term off heat

____

7. Leeve like that for 25 minute

____

8. Run cold water over egs

____

9. Peal.

____

PURCHASING PROBLEM!

Paddy Pantry is the purchaser for "The Cooking With Carmen Show." Each Friday Carmen gives Paddy a list of items she will need for the following week's shows. Paddy tries to group the things on the list in categories to make his shopping easier. But he's misplaced some of the items. Proofread his list and re-group the items to help Paddy get organized.

SHOPPING LIST

Bakery

rye bread
2 rolls paper towels
1 lb. butter
1 bunch bananas

Produce

8 hot dogs
1 pt. sweet cream
1 head cabbage
1 stalk celery
2 onions
2 lbs. potatoes

Meats

2 lbs. ground meat
12 chicken legs
12 chicken wings
1/2 lb. bacon
1/2 lb. bologna

Miscellaneous

dish detergent
aluminum foil
1 lb. peanuts
mustard
mayonnaise

Canned Goods

1 box bandaids
1 dozen eggs
2 ears corn
4 oz. tuna

Frozen Food

salt
orange juice
   concentrate
fresh peas
1 qt. vanilla ice cream
small vanilla extract

Dairy

8 oz. cling peaches
1 qt. milk
8 oz. American cheese
1 can tomato soup
3 oz. cream cheese

Staples

5 lbs. flour
5 lbs. sugar
1 lb. noodles
large cocoa
small honey

SHOPPING LIST

Bakery

Produce

Meats

Miscellaneous

Canned Goods

Frozen Food

Dairy

Staples

Proofing is in the Pudding © THE MONKEY SISTERS, INC.

T.V. TIMES

Mr. Potts, the home economics teacher, has posted this week's schedule for "The Cooking With Carmen Show." Proofread these clippings from the *T.V. Times* and copy them over correctly.

— Monday —

Noon ① *Cooking With Carmen Show*

Today is snack day. Carmen prepares cheese wafers and cheese popcorn.

____

____

____

____

— Tuesday —

Noon ① *Cooking With Carmen Show*

 Carmen present's holiday cooking on today's show. She'll be making pumkin cookies and witches brew. Her speshal guess is Broom Hilda.

____

____

____

____

— Wednesday —

Noon ① *Cooking With Carmen Show*

Easy meals are featered on Carmen's show. How to cook a healthly stew is highlighted? Guess appearances made bye a local 7th grade class.

____

____

____

____

— Thursday —

Noon ① *Cooking With Carmen Show*

 A special treat is in store on today's show. Carmen gives birthday advise. She bakes and easy but beuatiful brithday cake.

____

____

____

____

— Friday —

Noon ① *Cooking With Carmen Show*

Shoping hints are highlighted on the cooking show. Using coopons and carefull and wise buget planing are disgusted. Carmen's guess is A.P. Shopright.

____

____

____

____

ANNOUNCING
CARMEN'S COOK-ALIKE CONTEST

Here are some previous winners of this fabulous contest.
Follow the rules carefully and you too may be a lucky winner!!

Rules:

1. Choose a category: Breakfast Dessert
   Lunch Snack
   Dinner Beverage

2. Write your recipe (incorrectly) on the card below. (Use an extra sheet if necessary.)

3. Have a classmate proofread it and copy it correctly on a second recipe card.
   (Use an extra sheet if necessary.)

4. Submit your entry to your teacher by ___________________.
   date

5. Awards will be given by your teacher for each recipe category and for perfect proofreading.

6. Awards will be based on originality and neatness of recipe and for care in proofreading.

- -

OFFICIAL ENTRY BLANK

A Recipe by: _______________________   Proofread by: _______________________

Category: _______________________

____

____

____

____

____

____

____

____

   Proofing is in the Pudding © THE MONKEY SISTERS, INC.

1st Prize!!
Carmen's Cook-Alike Contest
Best Wake-Up Breakfast

Student ______________________

Teacher ______________________

Date ______________________

1st Prize!!
Carmen's Cook-Alike Contest
Above Average Beverage

Student ______________________

Teacher ______________________

Date ______________________

1st Prize!!
Carmen's Cook-Alike Contest
A Luscious Lunch!

Student ______________________

Teacher ______________________

Date ______________________

1st Prize!!
Carmen's Cook-Alike Contest
Winner of a Dinner!!

Student ______________________

Teacher ______________________

Date ______________________

1st Prize!!
Carmen's Cook-Alike Contest
The Most Snappy Snack.

Student ______________________

Teacher ______________________

Date ______________________

1st Prize!!
Carmen's Cook-Alike Contest
Your Just Desserts

Student ______________________

Teacher ______________________

Date ______________________

Proofing is in the Pudding © THE MONKEY SISTERS, INC.

MAKE-A-GOOD-GLOSSARY

As a special service to our viewers, the staff of "The Cooking With Carmen Show" has prepared the following glossary of cooking terms. A copy of this glossary will be sent free to any viewer who requests one by sending us a postcard.

The writer made some errors in spelling these words, so please proofread the glossary for me. Copy the word and the definition correctly onto the blank 'Make-A-Good-Glossary' pages.

GLOSSARY OF COOKING TERMS

Beet: To make a mixcher smothe by adding air with a brisk whiping motion useing a spoon or a electric mixer.

Blend: To throughly combine to or more ingredants by stiring.

Biol: To cook in liqud at boiling temprature (212 °F or 100 °C).

Bouillon: A cleer soap maid by cooking meet with vegtables and seasonings than straining the stock.

Broil: To cook by direct heet under a broilor.

Chop: To cute into peices abuot the size of peas.

Coat: To evenly cover whith crums, flour, ect.

Cool: To remove from heet and let stand at room temprature.

Cube: To cut into pieces that are the same size on eeach side—at lest 1/2 inch.

Dot: To put small bits of food over anohter food.

Dust: To sprinckle foods lightly whith sugar, fluor, ect.

Fold: To ad engredants gentle to a mixter.

Freeze: To reduce the temprature of food so a liquid becomes a solad.

Fry: To cook in hot fat.

Marinate: To alow a food to stand in liquid to add flaver.

Peal: To remove the skin from a fruit or vegtable.

Reduce: To boil rapidly so the liquid evaperates.

Shred: To rub food on a shreder to form long, thin pieces.

Sift: To put dry iengredients throug a sifter to brake up chunks.

Simmer: To cook in liquid over low heet.

Stir: To mix whit a spoon.

Toss: To mix by lifting and droping.

Proofing is in the Pudding © THE MONKEY SISTERS, INC.

MAKE-A-GOOD-GLOSSARY

Proofing is in the Pudding © THE MONKEY SISTERS, INC.

CURLS FOR CARMEN?

Cookie Croissant has been hired as the new hairstylist on
"The Cooking With Carmen Show." Naturally, when Carmen
mailed Cookie the directions, they were all mixed up. Help
Cookie find her way to the studio by reading the map and
numbering the directions in the proper order.

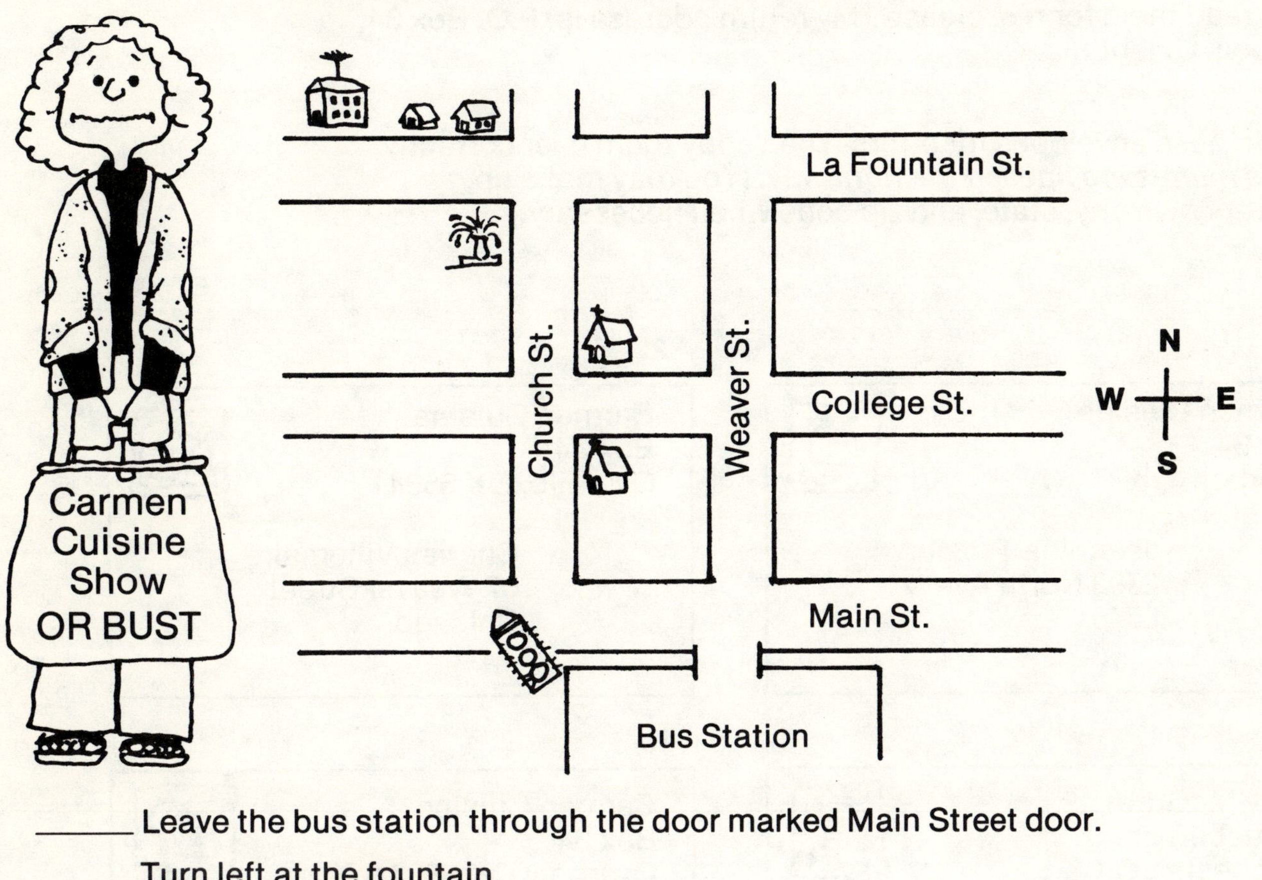

______ Leave the bus station through the door marked Main Street door.

______ Turn left at the fountain.

______ Take the bus to Main Street.

______ Turn left at Main Street and walk to the first traffic light.

______ Check in with the receptionist.

______ Turn right onto Church Street. Walk for two blocks past the twin churches.
Stop when you see the fountain on the corner of Church and La Fountain streets.

______ The studio is the third building on the right — 1400 La Fountain.

Answers: 2, 5, 1, 3, 7, 4, 6.

MIXED UP MAIL

Welcome back to "The Cooking With Carmen Show." Many of my viewers have been writing in to ask me for copies of the fabulous recipes we prepare on the show. I have answered all of these requests promptly, but for some reason all these letters were returned to me undelivered. I must have made a tiny error that I can't see. Will you proof read them for me, please? My return address is: P.O. Box 34, Overboil, Oklahoma.

Check these envelopes for errors. Then copy them over correctly. *All the names are spelled the right way.* (You may make up your very own city, state, and zip code when necessary.)

1.

Carmen Cuisine
Box 34
Overboil, OK

Jeannine Tessier
2793 North Ave.
65401

2.

Carmen Cuisine
Box 34
Ovrebilo, OK 65341

Charles Villemaire
67 Weaver Street
Chicago

3.

Mary McGrath
6 Bluebird Ln.
Colchester, OK
65347

Carmen Cuisine
Box 34
Over Boil, OK

4.

Carmen Cuisine
Box 34
Overboil, OK 65341

Peggy Blanchette
P.O. Box
Monkton Ridge, OK

5.

Frederick Lesson
207 North Ave.
Burlington, OK

Carmen Cuisine
Box 34
Overboil, OK 65341

6.

Carmen Cuisine
Box 34
Overboil, OK 65341
November 15, 198-

Nora Culhane
Waterbury, OK
24 Maple Ave.

   Proofing is in the Pudding © THE MONKEY SISTERS, INC.

FIXED UP MAIL

Use this page to correct the envelopes that Carmen incorrectly addressed.

1.

2.

3.

4.

5.

6.

Sylvia Kelley Sloane has written this review of "The Cooking With Carmen Show" for next week's edition of the *Midville Chronicle*. Proofread her newspaper article and copy it correctly.

COOKING WITH CARMEN . . .
A DANDY TREAT
Sylvia Kelley Sloane

Sylvia Kelley Sloane teaches at the Classical Cooking College. She also critiques recipes for national food magazines.

There is a television show currently broadcasted on Chanel XYZ TV which this reviewer finds outstanding and worthwhile. It is called "The Cooking With Carmen Show." Carmen offers delicious, nourishing and easy recipe's to delite everyones tastebuds. She is energetic and refreshing. There is never a dull momint on this show. Carmen add's extra spice and zing to the variety of food's she prepare's. Every show is a picnick full off tasty fun.

Tune in and treat yourself too this extraordinary cooking show scene daily at 12:00 P.M.

____
____
____
____
____
____
____
____
____
____
____
____

 Proofing is in the Pudding © THE MONKEY SISTERS, INC.

MAKE-AN-'M'-MENU

One of the stagehands asked me to do her a favor and prepare a special menu for her daughter, Mary Margaret's birthday. She said she wanted all the food served at the luncheon to start with the letter 'M.'

Please proofread the menu before we print them!

MARY MARGARET'S MENU

Apetizer: Marrinated mushrooms on mini-muffins
                    or
              Minestone soup with Melba toast

Entre: Meatballs a la miason
                    or
              Milk-fed veal magnifique
              Mashed potatos a la Carmen

Desert: Maccaroons with chocolate morsles
              Milk

When you re-write the menu correctly, please do so in your very best handwriting on the menu below. If it's fancy and beautiful, we can use yours!

THE PROOF AND MOVE GAME

This game is for 2-4 players and 1 game leader.

Directions:

1. Each player, in turn, rolls one die.
2. Player moves the number of spaces on the die.
3. Player proofreads the sentence in the space on which he/she landed.
4. Player tells the leader how many errors are in the sentence.
5. Leader checks the answer sheet below.
6. If player is correct, he/she stays in the space. If incorrect, the player must move back the number rolled on the die.
7. First player to reach 'Finish' is the winner.

Enrichment: The game can be made more challenging by requiring the players to correct the errors in the sentences.

Answer Key for Game Leader:

1. Four	9. Nine
2. Five	10. Zero
3. Four	11. Three
4. Seven	12. Four
5. Nine	13. One
6. Four	14. Six
7. Zero	15. Four
8. Seven	16. Two
	17. Three

Corrected Sentences:

1. The chef got his finger stuck in the bread dough.
2. The chicken was almost done when the electricity went off.
3. All of a sudden, the oven door opened.
4. Mrs. Yoke is baking us a special treat of chocolate brownies.
5. Carmen got peanut butter and jelly on her shoulder and in her hair.
6. Herb drinks a lot of milk; sometimes as much as a quart a day.
7. Frederica Fudge never misses "The Cooking With Carmen Show."
8. Al Almond thought he had a good idea of what southern cooking was like until he tasted Carmen's cooking.
9. Lee and I made Chuck a pineapple pie for dessert last Saturday.
10. Patty and Peggy practiced peeling potatoes.
11. Eating your vegetables can help you grow to a great height.
12. Ruth Rarebit gave Mary Mince and I a second helping of dessert before we even asked for it.
13. David Dumpling didn't do the dishes.
14. Willie Wellington says you can stretch your food dollars by using rice, pasta, etc.
15. Joyce Gelatin just barely finished dinner when the company arrived.
16. Hope, Laura, and Carrie ate the whole pizza.
17. It's fun to eat warm waffles with syrup for breakfast.

 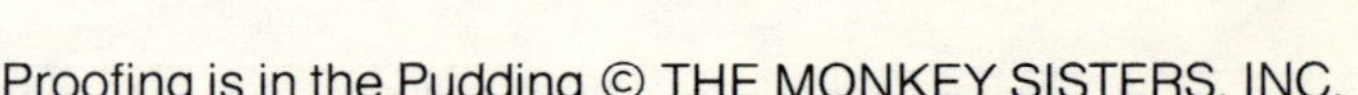 Proofing is in the Pudding © THE MONKEY SISTERS, INC.

THE PROOF AND MOVE GAME

Start

1. The chef gut his his fingur stucke in the bread doe.

2. The chichen were amost done when the electrisity went of.

3. All of the sudden, the ovan door opend

4. Mrs. yoke is backing us a speciale threat of chocolit brownys.

5. Carmen gut peenut buter on jellie on here soldier an in her heir.

6. Herb drinks a lot of milk, somtimes as mutch as a court a day.

7. Frederica Fudge never misses the Cooking With Carmen Show.

8. Al Almond though he had a good idear of what southren cookin was like untill he tasted Carmens Cooking.

9. Me and Lee maid Chuck, a Pinapple Pie for desert last saterday.

10. Patty and Peggy practiced peeling potatoes.

11. Eating your vegetibles can help you grow to a grate heighth.

12. Ruth Rarebit gave Mary Mince and I a second helping of desert befor we evan ask for it.

13. David Dumpling did'nt do the dishes.

14. Willie Wellington say you can strech your food dollars by using rise, pastah, ect.

15. Joyce Gelatin just baerly finished diner when the companys arived.

16. Hope, Laura, and Carrie eight the hole pizza.

17. Its fun to eat warm waffels with sryup for breakfast.

Finish

Blank extras

Name

Name

Proofing is in the Pudding © THE MONKEY SISTERS, INC.

Progress in Proofing

Well done!

Medium well done!

Needs more time!

Rare, but a good beginning

Not cooking yet!

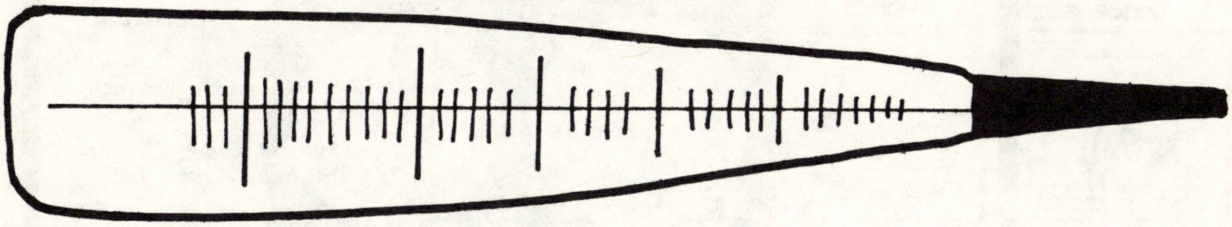

Student: _____________

Teacher: _____________

Date: _____________

Proofing is in the Pudding © THE MONKEY SISTERS, INC.

Now You're Cooking!!!

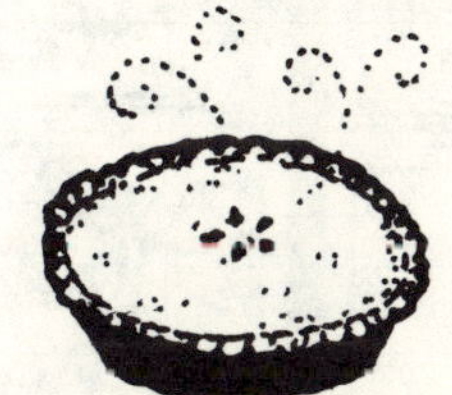

This is to certify that

____

is a very careful worker
and can correct and cook!

Teacher _______________________________ Date _______________

Proofing is in the Pudding © THE MONKEY SISTERS, INC.

See your local school supply dealer for these products by THE MONKEY SISTERS